New Island / New Drama

A Night in November

In the same series:

Long Black Coat — John Waters

A NIGHT IN NOVEMBER

Marie Jones

New Island Books / Dublin
Nick Hern Books / London

A Night in November
is first published in 1995
in Ireland by
New Island Books,
2, Brookside,
Dundrum Road,
Dublin 14
Ireland
& in Britain by
Nick Hern Books,
14 Larden Road,
London W3 7ST.

Copyright © Marie Jones, 1995

ISBN   1 874597 24 3 (New Island Books)
       1 854592 58 0 (Nick Hern Books)

New Island Books receives financial assistance from
The Arts Council (An Chomhairle Ealaíon),
Dublin, Ireland.

All rights whatsoever in this play are strictly reserved,
and application for performance should be made, before
rehearsal, to A.P. Watt, 20 John Street,
London WC1N 2DR.

Cover design by Jon Berkeley
Cover photo of Dan Gordon as Kenneth McCallister
by Jill Jennings
Typeset by Graphic Resources
Printed in Ireland by Colour Books, Ltd.

R 52209

A Night in November was first produced by **DubbelJoint Productions** at The West Belfast Festival, Whiterock, BIFHE, Belfast on the 8th of August, 1994. The cast was as follows:

KENNETH McCALLISTER   Dan Gordon

Director   Pam Brighton
Design   Robert Ballagh

Production Manager   Guy Barriscale
Stage Manager   Kevin Sullivan

DubbelJoint Administrator   Justin Binding

ACT ONE

The setting and props are minimal. The back drop is a representation of a football crowd; the staging is a rostra which has three levels representing the terrace.

The rostra is painted red, white and blue which flips to green, white and orange when Kenneth reaches Dublin airport. The only props are a World Cup T-shirt, shorts and hat. The actor moves around the stage creating the environment and plays all the characters without the aid of other props or additional scenery. The actor creates sound effects when necessary.

As lights come up, Kenneth McCallister, a minor civil servant in his thirties, walks onto the stage. Further stage directions at the discretion of the director.

KENNETH: That day started out like every other day starts out...check under the car for explosive devices...you have to be a step ahead of them bastards...they keep advancing their technology, gone are the days of the good old fashioned learnt at their mother's knee trip wire attached to the ignition, now they can blow you up with a device no bigger than a box of matches...they'll not get me...then out she comes, I see her feet coming at me from where I'm lying under the car...advancing on me, like two great black patent rottweilers, I watch them as they come to rest just in my eyeline, I glare at them, they glare back, I take them on...look them straight in the eye and wait.

For dear sake Kenneth, who would want to blow you up?

I am a government employee.

You're only a dole clerk, Kenneth, will you catch yourself on.

(He mimics her.) You're only a dole clerk Kenneth, only a dole clerk, Kenneth, only a glorified charity worker, pen pusher, not even a real dog, a bloody poodle or one of them other skittery wee mongs that only

7

shit in litter trays, not even a real dog, not even important enough to be on a hit list...bastards.

Daddy can I go with you and Granda Ernie to the football match?

NO...

Daddy can I go then?

NO...

If he's not takin' me he's not taking you, isn't that right Daddy?

No...

Then that means you're takin' me?

No...

But you said you weren't taking him if you're taking me which means you are taking me...

No, you're not going, I don't want to go, but I have to take Granda Sixty Cigarettes A Day Ernie because Granda Polluted Lungs can't go on his own and Mammy in her wisdom has instructed Daddy to take Granda Nicotine because Granda can't get up the steps on his own because he has inflicted early death on himself so thank you very much Mammy.

You don't like my father do you...?

NO.

(*Jumps out of the car.*)

Ah, good morning, Box D and how are you...

Dead on Kenneth...

And what have we this morning, Box D?

A Fresh Claim Kenneth.

Aaggh Fresh Claims. I love Fresh Claims...love it love it love it love it.

(*Sits down.*)...Next.

Fill that in...and sign there.

Where?

There.

Sorry, where...?

There...do you see where I have put that big gigantic X, that huge big black enormous X, that great big hulk of an X which I put there to make sure you sign in the right place...there...Patrick McCardle... Dependents...?

Six.

Children?

Aye...fuck sake what else wud they be.

Six children?

Aye, wud have been seven but she lost one...you know.

Oh dear...

Available for work from today?

...Yes...

...Yes?...

Yes...

Good, you'll be wanting family income supplement, eh, I'll give you an appointment for...tomorrow a.m.

...Sure I'm here now...

So?

So can I not see them people now...

So am I...

So are you what?

Here now but I have to come back tomorrow don't I?

Aye, but I won't be here...I have to go to Dublin.

(Writes.) Not available for work as out of the country.

What...I'm only going to Dublin for the morning.

You're out of the country.

I'm going out on the eight o'clock and back on the 11 o'clock, I'm only taking my oul ma down to meet her sister who is meeting her at the station.

You're out of the country.

I'm not gettin' off the train I'll only be helping her onto the platform.

The train will be in a foreign country and you will be on it and technically speaking you are not available for work as you are out of the country.

Standing on a platform?

A foreign country platform.

I'm available for work until I get to Newry which will be about nine then on the way back I'll get to Newry about twelve. So, I'll only be out of the country for three hours...so if I tuk my lunch break, two tea breaks and two toilet breaks altogether and worked a half an hour over-time I could go to a foreign country and back and do a day's work so what's the problem sunshine...

Right, you want an appointment do you...for today, sir...that should be no problem if you would just like to take a seat and I shall call you at the first available appointment...you don't mind waiting sir...just over there *(He watches him go.)* Just over there where I can watch you waiting and waiting and waiting you clever bastard. Sorted that one out Box D, didn't I...

You did Kenneth.

Trying to make a mug of me.

He was Kenneth.

We know how to sort the feckless hallions out, don't we Box D?

We do Kenneth.

By my reckoning there won't be another appointment until at least tomorrow, but I am going to enjoy you waiting Mr. Smart Ass...yes Audrey, I will have a cup of tea and two jammy dodgers please...what...why not, he usually takes custard creams, so he just decided to have one of the only two remaining jammy dodgers because he knows I like them, that's why...I'll remember that, and you tell him Audrey that Kenneth Norman McCallister will remember that...Next.

A Night in November

(Lifts phone.)

I told you before Debrah, don't phone me at work, Jerry doesn't like it...what...what does it say...honest, I've been accepted...no kidding Debrah...that's fantastic...me, they have accepted me, I can't believe it...it's an honour alright, they are all doctors and bank managers and God knows what...what do you mean don't let you down, what do you think I'm gonna do...we are all the same on the golf course love...I'll bet you it was because at that second interview I said Philip Morgan comes to our house for dinner, wait until I tell Jerry Duffy, he has been trying to get accepted for two years now...Jesus, I can't wait to see his face...*(Whispers.)* It's because he's a Catholic but the club can't admit that, but he knows and you and I know but nobody can prove it...get off the phone love, I have to go into his office and tell him...there's the laugh, he is the supervisor and he can't get accepted...that's one up for me, love, brilliant...see you later.

(Puts the phone down.)

Jerry, I just left those files on your desk I have dealt with them like you asked...oh, by the way, fancy a game of golf on Sunday.

Sunday is a tough day to get on the course if you're not a member, Kenneth.

(Out front.) I have waited for years for this moment but I must act casual...I don't want him to feel inferior, now control yourself Kenneth, it's all in your stride...right...here goes...

Well actually Jerry, that should not be a problem because I have just been accepted as a member and as a member, you will be permitted as long as you're with me...I'll call you later to arrange the time.

I had to get out, had to go straight out, straight out to the toilet and laughed.

I couldn't bear to look back at the envy on his face, the years of gloatin', with that "I got the post over a Protestant" look wiped off his face...because Jerry son, whether you like it or not, you'll never be one of us, at the end of the day, when the chips are down, when hardy comes to hardy, even when the fat lady sings we will always stick to our own...me a member of the Golf Club, him my boss and him having to kowtow to me to get on the course...things are looking up for Kenneth Norman McCallister...member of the Club.

A Night in November

(Opens the car door and winds the window down.)

Wind your window down Ernie would you please...I know it's November, Ernie, but you also know Ernie, November or not I don't allow smoking in the car and seeing as how you can't go five minutes without a cancer stick, Ernie, you will have to contend with the November winds...so you have two choices, freeze and smoke or be warm and stick a patch on...

I don't like football Ernie, so I hope you appreciate this.

Don't like football, you're not a man at all...I worry about you.

Do you Ernie, well did you know that your daughter is the wife of a man who has been accepted into the Golf Club, tell that to your cronies in the Buff Club.

Golf...that's an oul doll's game, the men in the Buffs wouldn't be impressed by that, tell you what, you come down with me and buy them a drink and that would impress them, that's if they let ye over the door...they haven't forgive me for lettin' my daughter marry a dole clerk...I was called a traitor...I nearly think it wud have been better if she'd married a Fenian, be more acceptable...The scourge of Ulster is what yis are known by down in our club. I have watched grown men reduced to wee childer by yis...them men shouldn't have to beg for money of youse clients, them is decent men who are out doing a day's work to feed their childer.

If they are out doing a day's work then they shouldn't be down at the dole, that's the problem.

(Shouts out the window.)...Go away back to your own country.

What did you shout, Ernie.

That car that just passed has a Free State reg on it...Pope lovers comin' up here.

So what, Ernie, they are up to see the match...support their team.

Support a shower of half-baked Fenian lovers...I'd luk over it if they were real Irish, but sure for Jesus sake the half of them's English that weren't good enough to play for England and then they discover some oul Irish bog woman that was meant to be their granny, they never set fut in Ireland before, wouldn't have known a shelalaigh from a hole in the wall and now, be Jesus, you'd think they started the 1916 Easter Rising.

Oh, so it would be alright if they were here supporting real Irish.

No, it wouldn't but I'd luk over it.

Our Debrah was telling her Ma that now that you're a member of the Golf Club, we can all go for a wee drink on Sunday afternoons and take the kids...her Ma is all chuffed, she has Freemans' club book out already pickin' a frock, they are all doctors and bank managers and what have ye, says she...so I says to her, I'll be nice to a doctor when I'm sick and civil to a bank manager when I'm lukin' for a loan but when we are all drinking together I am as good as any man...aye drink is a great oul leveller. *(He spits.)*

It's 16 and 17 Ernie, they're over here.

Aye, we'll show the dirty Fenian bastards.

Aye, no surrender.

Is this a football match Ernie, or a crowd of lions waiting for the Christians...what's going on here.

They've got blood in their nostrils Kenny, Fenian blood, worse than that foreign Fenian blood and what's even more despicable than that, mercenary Fenian blood...here they come, here's our boys...*(Chants.)* Northern Ireland, Northern Ireland, come on lads show them Papish bastards how to play fut ball...luk, luk, there's Billy...*(Shouts.)* Billy Bingham for king *(Sings.)* We love you Billy, we love you, so just tell them bastards where to go ...that's our boys the Billy Boys, no problem...

Luk at them, luk at them dirty Fenian scum...BOO

(Ernie sings.) God save our gracious Queen etc. etc.

(During anthem.)...Makes ye proud to be British when you hear that Kenny son, luk our boys standing to attention, luk at the Republic team...moving about, luk at them moving about, make them stand still.....make them...make them...look at them having to stand there, serves them right that they have to stand for ours and we are not playing theirs...serves them right because it is our country and them is all Fenian hallions...SEND HER VICTORIOUS...

Ernie, I must point out that that is the English national anthem and the ones who are not English live there anyway, so I am sure that it does not disturb them one way or the other and that all they want to do is play a game of football...well that was a red flag to a bull if ever there was one.

Oh, does it not, does it not, well let me tell you they may luk like mere innocent futball players but as far as I am concerned they are representing the I.R.A. get it...the Irish Republican Army, understand, Republic of Ireland, same thing, if they are prepared to sully themselves by playing under the banner of the Republic of Ireland I don't give a shite, if they are from Stoke on Trent or bloody Blackpool because to me they are representing the men that blow up our peelers or kill our soldiers...and what is more, as far as the Protestant people of this province is concerned, they are...Fenian scum.

Dirty Fenian scum...*(Chants.)* There's only one team in Ireland.

Come on lads, get stuck into them dirty Taigs.

(Starts to grunt.) uh uh uh uh...come on boys kick the ballicks off that big gorilla...where's your spear, you big ape ye...

Ernie.

What's wrong with ye, sure they're fucking black aren't they?...luk, three black men...*(Shouts.)* Hey, where did you get your players...the zoo? *(Laughs.)*

Then all around me...

Trick or Treat, Trick or Treat, Trick or Treat, Trick or Tre...

Hear that Kenny, hear that, our boys miss nothin'...*(Laughs, then shouts.)* Greysteel seven, Ireland nil...do da do da...hey listen Kenny, listen...they're all at it now, Greysteel seven, Ireland nil, do da do da day...hey, I started that one and now thousands has joined in, it was me that started it, me Ernie Thompson, magic.

Greysteel seven, Ireland nil, Greysteel seven, Ireland nil...

I felt sick, I felt such shame...ashamed of him, ashamed that I'd married someone who came from him, ashamed of standing in the same place as men like him...it's beyond words, it's beyond feeling...I'm numb...Greysteel seven Ireland nil...trick or treat...men walk into a pub on Halloween, shout Trick or Treat and mow down seven innocent people and these fuckin' barbarians are laughin'...surely to God, surely to Christ these are not the people I am part of...no, it's not, don't tell me, I'm not hearing them, I'm not for I can't fucking handle it...Then I started.

Ernie, you are low life at its lowest, you are the foulest human being that I have ever had the misfortune to know...you know if you were dead I wish I could be the first maggot to eat at your festered brain...the first worm to bore into your stinking heart, the first dog to shite on your grave and the last person to see you alive because then I could say all this to you, but I can't Ernie, because I look around me and there are hundreds of Ernies and I am numb...

Then I could see a couple of men looking at me not chantin' and I got scared so I started to open my mouth and close it like I was saying what they were saying...then I clocked the man beside me...I knew he was a Republic supporter because he had his head buried hoping he wouldn't be spotted not chantin' or cheering and I wanted to say...me being nice to a Catholic for no good reason...I wanted to say, luk, at me I'm only opening my mouth and closing it, do what I'm doing and you will be alright, but Ernie was getting over-excited, more obscene and God, I wanted to grab the man beside me and run him out of the place with my hands over his ears...then a goal...a goal for Northern Ireland and the place erupts and the man beside me stands up and claps desperate not to give himself away.

You're not going to the USA, doo da, doo da...

This is not a football match, it's a battle field, it's not about who wins, it's about who doesn't win...please God, make it a draw.

Dirty turncoat...luk at that Lundy...Lundy...Lundy...That wee bugger was born here and now luk at him playing for the Fenians...kick the wee bollick's shite in.

Get me home get me out of this...the crowd in front started to sing the Sash and Ernie'd joined in with great gusto, then a dig in the ribs from Ernie.

Join in, do you want the lads to think you're a half-baked Prod or somethin'...sing.

And I sang, spitting the words out...spewing out the words of a song that I grew up with that I'd sung with such passion so many times and now the words and the tune seemed so despicable.

And the Republic scores and there is a deathly silence apart from the players who are not even sure they scored because no-one is cheering...the Republic supporters desperate not to give themselves away stand in silence hoping no-one can detect any signs of pleasure on their faces, and the Billy Boys are silenced for a moment as their cold eyes scour the grounds looking for the one Irish supporter who can't control his feelings, and the man beside me can't cheer or clap he just looks blank hoping to God he has no signs of joy on his face...frightened to clap he just stares straight ahead, I look at him and he looks away...I nudge him and whisper out of the side of my mouth 'Well done mate'...I had this great rush of adrenalin when I said it...the man didn't respond, probably thought, it's a trick they want me to give myself away...of course he thought that, why would he trust me in the company of Ernie, delirious with hate.

And the Sash My Father Wore starts up again, just to show the Billy Boys won't be silenced for long...and the crowd of men in front look at the man beside me and I hear the poor man beside me sing it, trying desperately to fight for the words and I sing it in his ear, not to provoke him, but to help him...he realises I am not his enemy and he trusts me.

And then the final whistle...the man beside me rushed away with his head down...desperate to escape as if he had just committed a crime...I wanted to go after him...

Come on Ernie this way.

Houl on, houl on, no rush.

The game is over, come on.

You want people to think we are not proud of our boys...do you want to sneak off as if them dirty Pope lovers got the better of us...I'll tell you what, if I was a fitter man, the first smug lukin' Freestater I saw would be picking his Fenian teeth out of my boots...*(Shouts.)* Trick or Treat.

I drove home that night with the dreaded Ernie...I wanted to scream, wanted to stop the car and throw him out...but did I...no, I sat there and listened and hadn't the bottle to challenge him...no, too many years of accepting what Ernie accepted, so I sat in silence, knowing in my guts that Ernie had to be wrong, but Jesus Christ, where does that leave Kenneth Norman McCallister.

A Night in November

And as he took another gulp of air I prayed to God that it would be his last, but no fear.

You know what, Kenny, I don't care if them Fenians are gettin' to go to the World Cup, sure they'll get bate anyway...aye, let them go back to Ireland bummin' and blowing that they are going to America but as far as I am concerned we showed them...good night.

What can you say, what can you say to a man like Ernie, sixty-five years of good old loyal bigotry, sixty-five years of salt of the earth racism, and sixty-five years of being at the bottom of the heap, look at him, can hardly walk, hardly breathe, fifty years of smoking himself to death but tonight Ernie is a happy man, because tonight Ernie got the chance he has been waiting for all those years...to express himself...God help us all.

I turned on the car radio...I heard a player being interviewed after the match...an English man, born in England of an Irish mother telling the commentator as he stood in Windsor Park in Belfast that he was happy for all his fans back in Ireland...back in Ireland?...where did he think he was...now while this man who was born in England, was playing football for the Republic, in Belfast, he was called a dirty Fenian Irish bastard and to go back to his own country...now on the other hand a player who was born in Belfast playing for Northern Ireland was also called a dirty Fenian Irish bastard because he was accused of playing too loose, because he was a Fenian in the first place.

(Gets out of the car.)...She's waving at me out the window, she never waves at me out the window...she's been watchin' and waiting for me because tonight she is proud of me...tonight I am not only a dole clerk...tonight I am a member of the Golf Club and at last she can up her status at aerobics.

Kenny, love, Valerie and Kyle say congratulations, Lisa and Malcolm want to buy you a drink and Pauline and Stuart pretended to be chuffed but I could sense as soon as I told Pauline that she was dead jealous...you'd know she was because as soon as I told her there was a few seconds silence, before she said Oh, Debrah, I am delighted for you. She was just the same when I told her Philip Morgan was coming to our house for dinner.

I have never witnessed such a despicable display of hatred as I have tonight.

A Night in November

I can imagine...anyway, wait til you hear this, Pauline is going to get her Mummy to knit you a sweater, you know the ones with golfers on and the best about it is she only knits those for ones that are actually members of clubs, she has this wee thing about only doing it for ones that are proper members.

They were shoutin' Trick or Treat, how can people stoop so low...

They are all scum, one side is as bad as the other, pay no heed to them...the kids don't mind that they can't get the new computer, I sat them down and said Daddy is a member of the Golf Club and it's a big thing...

Debrah, I am talking about your father, your father was ranting and raving like a man possessed with hatred, and...and...racism and...bigotry...

Don't mind my daddy, he always gets carried away at football matches...anyway, tell me what Jerry said...I bet he was livid, you got your own back, didn't you, let's have a glass of wine, we still have a bottle left over from last Christmas.

I cracked...

Listen you stupid empty-headed bitch, I don't want Jerry to be livid, do you know that, I don't want Jerry to feel like shit, I don't want him to go home to his wife and kids knowing that I am out to get him for no other reason than he is a Catholic...isn't that pathetic...but you don't want your husband to be pathetic...you want your husband to be a man and stand by his beliefs like your disgusting father, you don't care about nothin' only me wearing a stupid idiotic bloody sweater with a knitted golfer hittin' a knitted golf ball with a knitted fucking golf club.

But I didn't ...I said nothing because there are thousands of Debrahs married to thousands of Kenneths and I hadn't the balls to be the Kenneth that takes on the Debrah...how could I blame her, how could I when I didn't even know what I believed myself...I only knew that something was happening to me, but how could I face it, how could I stand there and look back at my whole life in one night...instead I had a glass of wine with my wife and tried to forget that awful night in November.

Ah, good morning Box D and what do we have today then?

The usual Kenneth.

A Night in November

Ah, the usual, how unusual.

Next.

You again...what happened, train strike?

No, you made me sit over there for two hours yesterday, knowing I had to come back anyway...I'm sure you sleep easy in your bed with the satisfaction of making people like me feel like shit. I want to tell you something mate, I have six kids, six kids and if I thought for one minute one of them was going to grow up and treat another human being the way you treated me yesterday, I would break their two legs to make sure they never worked...now just get on with it please because every minute I have to sit here and watch you looking at me like I am some kind of scum, the more I want to put my fist down your throat.

I had to get up, had to walk away...I looked into his eyes and I saw the years of acceptance of people like me treating him like dirt...years of accepting that he had to put up with my pathetic bigotry...years of knowing that because he was a Catholic, an out-of-work Catholic that he must accept being treated like he was nothing, of no worth and I looked into his eyes and I had to get up and walk away...he was right.

Excuse me would you, I'll get someone else to take over...sorry.

I stood in the middle of that office and looked round me. I watched myself sitting here for fifteen years, fifteen years of never looking into the eyes of anybody, thousands of faceless people with no eyes, no souls, no feelings, years of resentment and bitterness and pettiness and humiliation, just to make me, Kenneth McCallister a somebody. My head was spinning, I wanted to scream, wanted to jump up on the counter with a thousand giros in my hand and throw them at the people...here, go on, take the money, take the money and spend it on whatever you want, it doesn't matter, drink, horses, bingo, just go and have a good time on me...I watched myself do it...I felt I was standing there for hours just fantasising about what I could do if I wasn't a stupid little man, a stupid soul-less little prick...if it was even possible to change...was it...is it.

Audrey, I don't care if he ate the last jammy dodger the day again, you know that, I don't bloody care if he turns into a jammy dodger, just give me anything you have and I don't want tea today, I will have coffee, black coffee.

A Night in November

No, you're right, Jerry, I shouldn't have snapped at Audrey, I will go and apologise.

(He turns to walk away.)

I didn't know you liked football, Kenneth.

What, what did you say...what was that Jerry?

I saw you last night at the match but I was too far away to attract your attention. I never knew you liked football.

He looked at me, into my eyes...I felt like he had watched me commit a terrible crime...I'm sorry Jerry, I'm sorry, it wasn't me, you know that, it wasn't me, they don't speak for me, I was there and I was scared too, that's why you saw me opening and closing my mouth, but I swear to you Jerry, I said nothing, no Jerry don't think they speak for me...oh, but they do speak for you Kenneth, think about it Kenneth, think about the Golf Club Kenneth and you throwing it in Jerry's face Kenneth, think about the bitterness you felt because Jerry got that job and he wasn't a Prod, oh yes, Kenneth, they do speak for you, you're like them, you're one of them, you've always been one of them, so don't think that you can hide up in your nice semi and get away with it, don't think because you are member of the Club you can hide behind your hand-knit sweater and close your ears to them, because you are part of them...you can't escape so tell Jerry all that, go on, tell him...

I just had to take her Da...no interest myself...it was a bit scary, like, a bit hostile, I did notice that.

We all expected that, Kenneth, we were prepared for that.

Were you, Jerry?

Oh, aye.

Were you scared, Jerry?

Well, I wasn't exactly laid back about it, but as I say, we expected it...terrible pity, like, because it spoiled it for the players, they couldn't perform so it spoils it for everybody...pity...awful shame.

(Gets in the car.) I drove home with Jerry's words pounding in my brain...pity, he pities me, he pities me, who the fuck does he think he is, how dare he pity us, him that was trailed up in some Fenian gutter can sit there and pity me, pity my people...I saw myself in Windsor Park...I went back...I stood in the middle of the pitch and I shouted to

the hoards "Shut up, shut up to fuck, they are not frightened of you, they pity you, they are laughin' at ye, shut up, shut up, don't let them laugh at you."

...Trick or Treat...

Stop...stop...don't let them pity us...stop for fuck's sake, stop...you're a joke...stop...

Kenneth, look at this, it says...Congratulations on your success, and inside the card it says...To Kenneth, well done, from Pauline and Stewart and she has even drawn a wee golfer on it...really nice of them, wasn't it...it probably galled them but it was still thoughtful.

I looked at my wife, I looked at her and I said to myself "I don't love you, you have become a habit, like my jammy dodgers and my own special mug, we exist together."

You fancy going out for a meal tonight Debrah, get a baby sitter, go for a meal and a bottle of wine.

Are you right in the head, Kenneth?

Yes and I fancy going out for a meal.

There is something wrong, Kenneth, what is it?

I want to take you for a meal tonight, you and me, just us.

You have lost your senses...A, it is a Tuesday night, B, we could not afford it and C, you know I am on a diet, so for God's sake, Kenneth, get a grip.

I hate it, I hate when she does her ABCs, nothing is a yes or a no or a maybe, everythin' has to have an A and a B and a C, never just an A or even an A and a B...always three...always, always.

For once can you not answer me with an ABC, just for once Debrah, just once do somethin' that shocks me.

Will you for God's sake keep your voice down...the children...

Look at me Debrah, look at your husband, your loyal boring predictable husband and tell me, tell me do you love me.

There is something wrong with you...have you been drinking?

No Debrah, I have been thinking, for the past ten years...we haven't thought about anything that's worth a damn to anybody...all you think about is you and all I think about is me, and what is really important to us is what other people think about us, and those same people don't give two damns what we do or think because they are like us thinking only about themselves...so what is the point...what is the point, and if you say A, B or C, I will scream.

But she said nothing, she looked with desperate confusion in her eyes, 'I've lost my husband'...that's the look the poor girl had on her face, my husband is dead but he is standing lookin' at me...I wanted to hug her and comfort her and tell her it was alright. I looked at her sad little face the tears in her eyes, I saw the wee girl with her dolls in the pram dreaming of the white dress and the two children and the semi and the good loyal husband til death do us part...it didn't matter that she didn't love me really, Isobel doesn't love Ernie, Ernie doesn't love Isobel, but they exist together, why should I destroy all that for her.

She turned away from me, walked up the hall, lifted the youngest and held him tight to her, the bigger one held her hand.

Why are you crying Mammy?

(Quietly.) Daddy is cross with me

Then she said nothing, just held onto them quietly weeping, the eldest looked at me with his big sad accusing eyes and I had to get out, get away, get away from those eyes...I tried, but stopped and turned back.

Now, come on, Debrah, I'm sorry, go out into the garden kids and leave me and your Mammy...I'm sorry, Love.

Did you mean all that Kenneth.

No, I don't know what has come over me, I'm sorry, forget about it, forget I even said it...I'm just a bit pissed off with work and I took it out on you, that's all.

You're sure.

Yes, love.

And she smiled, not believing me, but knowing for the sake of her whole life, her whole existence that she must make herself believe me. She will make herself believe with the same will and determination that she does her step-ups in aerobics, with the same rigour that she cleans the house, the same dedication she puts into making sure her kids are going to pass the eleven plus, the same will power she has for sacrifice to better herself because it is all part of the same thing...all part of the same thing.

We are the perfect Prods, we come in kits, we are standard regulation, we come from the one design, like those standard kitchens with the exact spaces for standard cookers and fridges, our dimensions never vary and that's the way we want it, but what happens when the kit is put together and the appliances don't fit the spaces...what happens...chaos, mayhem and we can't cope, we can't cope.

From that moment on, I knew I had to stop, stop before it was too late, stop before I destroyed my wife and our put-upable little life. No, to look back now could only mean total disaster...so Kenneth McCallister vowed that night that he would never look back again.

I had to train myself not to think, not to see, just keep your head down and get on with it...I didn't want to hear the news or think about who I was and where I came from and what I was supposed to think, I didn't want to listen to the men I'd voted for, the Unionist politicians spouting on and saying nothing only "we won't budge, we won't change, we won't give in'...tried to imagine I was living in some insignificant little town in the middle of England, safe and surrounded and protected which was bearable until one night as I headed for the car after work...

Having problems with the car, Jerry?

Yeah, I'll go back in and ring a taxi.

I'll give you a lift home Jerry.

Why was I saying that, Jerry lived on the other side of town, bandit country, I'd never been there in my life, never had a desire to go there, but I was curious...I wanted to know beyond that man, where he lived, what his house looked like, what his wife looked like, what he had for his tea, what he thought about things...I couldn't ever imagine and for some daft reason I had to know, I wanted to know...I could hear the other Kenneth in my head, don't do it, don't do it, remember what you promised yourself, for the sake of your wife, your kids, your whole life, don't do it.

It's no problem, Jerry. Sure, she goes to aerobics and the kids are at their grannies on a Monday, so I've no need to rush home.

I drove up the Falls Road with Jerry, I had never been on the Falls Road in my life, never...the sun was shining, the road was hiving with black cabs and women and children and army tanks and normality and I was nervous, like a stranger in a foreign country, not sure of the territory, feeling like they were all looking at me, knowing I was a stranger, knowing I was the enemy but no-one paid a blind bit of notice, I fitted into the normality just like the soldiers...I felt a sudden rush of inexplicable anger...those soldiers look more at home here than me and this is my country...what was I saying...Jesus...then suddenly I began to laugh out loud.

If my wife could see me here now Jerry she would have a fit.

No kiddin'.

Never been up here in my life.

I've never been where you live in my life.

Funny, isn't it.

Yeah, weird.

And we drove in silence, what else could we say, funny, weird - that was what we said but what else could we say...two people who had worked together for fifteen years met on the golf course and yet two total strangers ...funny, ...yeah...weird.

Want to come in for a beer, Kenny?

I had pictured Jerry's house in my head, well, it couldn't be up to much I'd thought...he did live in West Belfast and we grew up with the pictures of deprivation and filth and graffiti and too many kids and not enough soap...well, there it was, bigger than mine...detached with a garage, the lawn strewn with bikes and scooters and toy tractors, strewn with life, not like ours, manicured to the last blade...the unwritten rule BIKES AND SCOOTERS FORBIDDEN EXCEPT ON THE CONCRETE PROVIDED...grey cold concrete especially laid so the kids wouldn't ruin the grass...the grass was for show, concrete could be scrubbed afterwards...and inside Jerry's house was a whole other life, a life I've never known, a life of disorder...books upside down in the bookcase, not in order of size or colour...in our house only properly bound ones went on show...Debrah's order from the book club...burgundy leather bound classics...never opened, but they suit the bookshelf, match the wallpaper, blend in with the carpet, books that can't be allowed to vary just like the fitted kitchens. I once wanted to order a couple of Stephen King's from the book club, unbound...No, Kenneth, we are not spending all that money on something that has to be hidden away in a drawer and I accepted it, of course I accepted it, God help me...and there in Jerry's house, books of all shapes and sizes, books that looked read had dog ears, piles and piles of them and I was jealous of Jerry and his disordered life and his higgledy-piggledy books.

'Fraid I can't offer you anything to eat, Kenny, I have to cook m'own the night, and I don't think that you would want to wait around while I burn it.

Wife not here, Jerry.

No, she's left a note on the kitchen table, she took a notion to take the kids to the pictures, so I'm to get my own.

Oh, God, what freedom, what wonderful unpredictability...and then at the bottom of the note which I strained my eyes to see, what Jerry never bothered to read out...Love You...why should he bother to read that out, it's a fact, it's unspoken, it's taken as read, but she still writes it, as a matter of course, just to make sure Jerry knows, but Jerry does know, so it doesn't matter if Jerry ever gets into the Golf Club because Jerry is loved by his wife, who still tells him...you lucky bastard, where did it all go wrong for me...where...how...why.

I drank the beer and left...I didn't want to go home, to be there when Debrah came in from aerobics...the woman I fell in love with had vanished into the perfect ten-by-ten square of our designed life, bound to the burgundy unopened classics and the scrubbed concrete...and me, her husband, the man she fell in love with tied to order and loyalty and nothing.

(Young boy's voice.)

Hey, mister, are you from the Branch?

What?

Are you lookin' for touts or somethin'?

I had driven from Jerry's to East Belfast, the street where I was born, where I had lived until my mother and father could escape from the smell of poverty and people like themselves, striving for the day when they could move to a place where they could close their door on it all, saving for the day when they could get Venetian blinds so that no one could ever look in on their lives or judge them ever again....they could judge Jerry and his kind from behind the secrecy of the blinds...bikes and scooters scattered over the lawn meant slovenliness, a pile of jumbled up books meant no pride or dignity in their lives, a wife who said cook your own tea meant low life at its lowest and all this meant second class, filth, scum and hatred...and I believed it.

The kid had wheeled his bicycle right up to the driver's window and was leaning it and himself on the car and poking his wee face in at mine.

No, I'm not the Branch...I used to live in this street...No. 34.

If you're not the Branch, what are you doing round here...

...Do you live here?

Aye...over there...my Da was born in this street too you know, and so was his Ma.

What's your Da's name?

He's dead.

Sorry son.

My Da is a hero, he got killed trying to blow up a Fenian pub...see, when I'm his age I won't get killed ...I'm not gonna miss, so I'm not.

What was your Da's name?

Norman Dawson...his photo's up on the wall of the club...he's dead famous...have ye any money on ye mister.

I gave him fifty pence and left...this time just driving away, I wanted out into the country away from people and their lives...

I had to think, I had to think about Norman Dawson...dead famous.

I sat looking into the river, the Lagan and thought of Norman Dawson. And I knew I couldn't go on pretending that I lived in the middle of England.

The river was dark and slimy and I stared and stared trying to see the bottom but years of silt and moss and pollution made it impossible. Maybe at one time it was clear...crystal clear, but never again.

Me and Norman were mates...Norman wanted to be a soldier...join the army, he was obsessed by killing Indians. I was always a sheriff, I enjoyed locking them up and torturing them. Norman always wanted them dead. One day they stopped being Indians and became Fenians, and Norman stopped being a cowboy and became a UDA commander in his Da's combat jacket...and I became a Special Branch man in m'Da's sunglasses...and we would play in Norman's house and his Da would laugh and encourage us, "how many Fenians did you kill the day, Norman, son'...thousands, so I did...dead on, son...I tortured them, Mr Dawson, so I did, I gave them some shit, so I did...stop that bad talk or I'll tell yer Ma...alright, I gave them some gip and then I tortured them...

We used to camp in his Ma's back yard, two feet away from the outside toilet...We'd lie, side by side, I knew every freckle on his face, every blackhead on his nose, we'd count them when we were bored waiting for our prey...perhaps Norman was just waiting for the day when he could really have someone to kill...no...no he wasn't a freak, a nutter, no, his picture is on the wall of the club and all the other Norman Dawsons who do it and get away with it and are hailed and become heroes...was I saved from being Norman Dawson by moving away to respectability and a couple of exams and a job that Norman hadn't...but are we that different...we all believed the same as Norman, but we couldn't dirty our hands killing Fenians, we were civilised so we closed our eyes and our Venetians and let Norman Dawson...we let Norman Dawson do it for us. Oh, yes, we showed our disgust, tutted loudly and then scurried back in to the ten-by-ten and never thought of Norman Dawson or his victims ever again.

You're home late, Kenneth.

Yes, Debrah...I gave Jerry a lift home and I went in and had a few beers with him.

You did what?

You heard.

Are you wise, going away up there...what was his house like?

Big.

Big? how big, big as this.

Bigger.

Bigger?...Detached?

Yeah.

I wonder how they managed that...what was his wife like.

She wasn't in, took a notion to take the kids to the pictures and told Jerry to see to his own tea.

Typical...poor fella, I suppose he is used to that behaviour.

Yeah, he is.

Disgustin', after the man does a day's work...was it tidy?

No.

You see, they manage to trail themselves out of the slums and then when they do get nice houses they let them go to wreck and ruin...is it any wonder, Kenneth?

Is what any wonder, Debrah?

Is it any wonder they don't deserve anything.

If you don't mind Debrah, I think I'll go and cut the lawn before it gets dark.

I hated my wife...I hated her so much, because she had echoed what I'd always thought, so I hated myself...before that awful night in November I accepted myself, put up with myself but what does a man do when he loathes himself?

END OF ACT ONE

ACT TWO

You wanted to see me Jerry.

I'm worried about you Kenny, you have been looking desperate this while back.

I'm alright, Jerry, honest.

You can talk to me.

Oh God, if only Jerry knew how much I wanted to talk to him but years of training on keeping yourself to yourself was a hard habit to break.

It's nothing Jerry...work gets you down sometimes, doesn't it.

Aye, sure, you'll be gettin' your holidays soon, going anywhere...

Debrah's mother's caravan in Ballyhalbert, we go every year.

That'll be nice.

Going anywhere yourself, Jerry.

...America, and I can't wait, I'll tell you...counting the days.

America.

The World Cup...Ireland's playing, remember...they say there won't be an American accent to be found in New York the week of the matches...Jesus, it will be like the Pope's visit without the Pope...but then I'm sure Ballyhalbert is good crack too.

That will cost a packet.

My wife's sister is over in New York, so we'll have somewhere to stay.

Your wife's goin' too.

It was her idea, she's mad. I kept saying we can't afford it, but she ignored me...Next thing I know she had the kids organised to stay with her mother and the tickets are booked...we were going to change the car but she just said to hell with it, sure there is no crack in that.

Does your wife like football.

No, she can't stand it, she just wants to see Ireland winning, she couldn't care less if it was bob sleighin' as long as Ireland won and she was there to cheer them on...I mean if you never liked futball the crack alone will be something else...

Sounds great.

Anyway, cheer up, and remember I'm here if you need me, Kenny.

Aye...and then out of the blue I asked him...

Jerry, why do you still live up there.

What?

You know, just wondering why you...you know...now, I hope you don't think I'm too nosey but I was just...well, it's been on my mind...the place is crawling with soldiers.

Why did I not buy myself out when I could...well, to be honest, Kenny, I feel safe there and I'm not sure if I would anywhere else...and I like the people, they're the ones I grew up with, so I put up with the soldiers...I know it's not ideal to go to work in the morning and trip over two squaddies crouched in your driveway...and you see your kids rushing past them munchin' away at their toast, but sometimes I look into those scared eyes looking up at me and sometimes I want to say "Look, this is bloody ridiculous, will you please come out from under my rhododendrum bush, it is bright lilac and youse are dressed in khaki, did youse learn nothing about camouflage", but you know, they have been told that we are the enemy...I thought I'd stop seeing them after a while, you know like living beside a railway line you stop hearing the trains, but I still see them...thank God.

Thank God?

Well, when I stop seeing them I suppose then I have accepted them...here I shouldn't be talking like this...I didn't mean to ramble on Kenny.

No it's alright Jerry...it's alright.

I went back to my desk and thought...yeah perhaps those squaddies under the rhododendrons were...ridiculous...how could I ever say that to anybody that I know? And then I began to feel envious of Jerry having the freedom to support Ireland, and I was jealous of that freedom - that he had something he believed in - how could I say that to anyone? I live in the same country and I am scared to mention that I envy him...for me, it was dangerous talk, for him, it's wild and wonderful crack...

I started to watch the news...I needed to know what was happening...every night there was speculation on the Downing Street Declaration...What was this...hope, change, could it be, would it be...and then the hoover would go on, she always puts the hoover on when politics are mentioned...

The news is on, the floor isn't dirty.

She can't hear because the hoover is on.

Yes...it was like that when I was growing up...as soon as the news came on my ma reached for the brush...automatic reaction...don't listen...just keep cleaning and everything will be alright...we have been protected by hoovers and dusters and brushes all our lives...

Kenny, you are in another world, sitting there. Will you put the nuts and crisps in a bowl, I have these vol-au-vents to fill.

(Ding, dong.)

Oh, my God, Kenny and I'm not prepared, they're here...I hate that, it's your fault, sitting there doing nothing and I have to do everything and now look at the state of the place and me like a right mess.

Debrah, you are perfect, there is not one hair out of place, not one speck of dust that hasn't been exterminated, everything is shining, so what the hell are you talking about.

I still have my flipping slippers on, don't I?

(Ding, dong.)

Well, take them off for Christ sake.

And you are standing with crisp bags in your hand...and I know it's Stewart and Pauline and I know she will take all in that we are not even prepared and she will love it.

Then why for God's sake do we have bloody friends like Stewart and Pauline who judge us on whether we have managed to put six packets of cheese and onion crisps in bowls.

Just shut up and answer the door...and don't let her come into the kitchen.

(Sarcasm.) Welcome, do come in, sorry we are not prepared but do have a drink...Debrah is just adding the finishing touches to things, sorry we aren't ready, but I was engrossed in the news. Well, I haven't seen you since the Declaration. What do you think, Pauline?

What?

The Declaration that everybody is talking about...the Downing Street Declaration.

Don't talk to Pauline about politics, Kenny, she hasn't a clue.

I do have a clue, Stewart, I know they can declare all they want but at the end of the day it smacks of sell-out to me and our politicians will never allow that to happen so it's a pointless exercise...enough of all that...we are here to enjoy ourselves...I have a present for you Kenny...well, seeing as this is a little celebration not only for your birthday, but for you getting into the Golf Club, I thought I'd mark it with these.

I wanted to laugh and scream at the same time...there they were, before my eyes, I held them and looked at them speechless...a set of knitted golf club covers with pom-poms on...red, white and blue knitted golf club helmets to keep my golf clubs warm, finished off with perfect little rounded fringed pom-poms, each little fringe exactly the same as the next...thousands of them...these must have taken up Pauline's mother's whole day.

Terrific, Pauline, condoms for my golf clubs...thank you, I am delighted about that, I was a bit worried about my eight iron and my putter. They were getting a bit close for comfort out on that green...I says right you two, no anky panky, unless it's safe sex, I don't want no wee putters running about.

She was not all that amused...Stewart was, he likes a dirty joke. He pulled me aside to tell me another one - Did you hear the one about the two nuns in the bath, one says wares the soap and the other says it does, doesn't it.

A Night in November

Out of the side of my eye, I see Pauline dart into the kitchen to wallow in my wife's unforgivable crime of failing to fill the vol-au-vents with mushrooms before eight o'clock...so I thought, tonight Kenneth, you may as well be hung for a sheep as a mushroom.

(Ding dong, ding dong, ding dong.)

Welcome, everybody, glad you could all come and help me celebrate thirty-four years of being an asshole but then I am in the right company.

...Laughs all round...they don't think I'm serious

I...would like to ask you if any of you were embarrassed by the football match that took place between Northern Ireland and the Republic of Ireland...

Confused looks all round...

No, you probably did not take it under your notice, of course you didn't. Why should any of us be interested or concerned that Ireland are through to the World Cup...well, most of us here aren't really into football.

More laughs, this time polite, but slightly nervous.

Well, let me tell you what you missed. I know it was a few months ago but you see it was one of those nights that is hard to forget.

Debrah's vol-au-vent is stopped in mid-air.

We are all respectable people here in this room and I am sure that if you had witnessed what I witnessed, heard what I heard, you would be as ashamed as me...of course you would.

No one is laughing now, dry embarrassed coughs, shuffling from foot to foot, hands reaching for crisps in an attempt to appear casual...a crisp falls on the floor... Debrah clocks it, but puts it to the back of her mind.

Yes, you would all have tut-tutted at this disgusting and ugly display of bigotry...you might even have been a bit embarrassed...but were you ashamed...I don't think so...is that because we can ignore those nasty low-lifes as not being part of us, yet we vote for the people who feed this evil. So why throw our hands up in horror when we hear of another loyalist murder committed by the men who fight and kill for Ulster, don't we all share Lord Carson's legacy don't we all still believe that this is ours, this our state and we must never give an inch. Don't they believe like us that we must keep those dirty Fenians down? Yes, it's alright not to employ them, alright to keep them out of the golf clubs, alright to screw up their benefits, but if you don't have the luxury of discriminating nicely and cleanly then what do you do, eh?...What do you do if you are a nobody and you still want to be part of Carson's army...you do what my friend Norman Dawson did, wipe them out in the only way you know how...why are you all looking so horrified...horrified at the thought that you might be classed as an ugly blood-thirsty barbarian. They are carrying out Carson's orders, they are defending the legacy, a legacy that left them nothing, defending it for us, so we can sit back and enjoy it...so at least have the decency to support them. If you don't, then for Christ's sake, come out and have the balls to condemn them...and condemn, not just what they do, but why they do it.

The silence was unbearable. I was aware of a pair of eyes boring through me, hard eyes that froze me to the spot. I felt I was jammed in the pupils, that if they blinked, I'd be pulverised...it was Pauline.

You are British and you should be ashamed of yourself.

Pauline, you are dead fucking right...I am.

Needless to say, after that terrible night in April, we had few phone calls from our friends. The word travelled fast that Kenneth had lost his marbles and was being brainwashed by Catholic workers in the D.H.S.S...I still checked under my car every day, but now I was scared of my own people...Debrah and I barely spoke, well, what do strangers say to each other...I suppose they find something, the weather, the price of beer etc. but those things seem ridiculous if the strangers are living in the same house, sharing the same bed and the same children. I'd gone too far, said too much. I should be ashamed of myself - I am British. So here I am on the island of Ireland being told to be ashamed for questioning our right to hate.

It's like we're living at the top of a bloody great big house and we think that we've got the best room, so we keep ourselves locked in, and we won't even open the door to let in fresh air. The air in the room is stale and we breathe it decade after decade, year after year, day after day and we are safe in our stale air.

Your Golf Club fees are due, Kenneth, don't forget.

This was how we continued our lives, we spoke when necessary, fed each other relevant information, talked a lot to the kids to cover silences...and at night, the unspoken rule of whoever goes to bed first, wait until the other is asleep before entering...that way it was bearable...this wasn't just a normal marital argument that could be patched up in a day or two when the heat died down...no, this did not need a patch, it was beyond patching, it was rendered obsolete, but we could not bear to deal with it.

Jerry was full of chat, one day at work.

Only a fortnight to go Kenneth...New York, here we come, Ole, Ole, Ole.

Yeah, sounds great crack, Jerry.

Twenty Aer Lingus flights leaving Dublin...they say there will be more people leaving Ireland that day, than did during the famine..I can't wait...be one big party from start to finish.

What if they don't win.

Since when would that stop us partying...the attitude will be, we didn't win, and we should have, so let's have a party to celebrate the fact that we could have, if we hadn't lost...know what I mean...

I wish Jerry wouldn't go on about America, I can't bear it.

Your Golf Club fees are a week late Kenneth.

Yes, Debrah, I am going to pay them soon.

I don't see why you left it so late, it's not as if the money is not there in the bank.

I do get one month to pay from the time of the invoice.

Yes, but I don't want them to think we have no money...or that we had to borrow it.

I am sure the accountant is not sitting thinking to himself, Kenneth must be in difficulties, oh dear, perhaps it was a bad idea to accept Kenneth as it is obvious he is not of the financial standing to be part of us...Debrah, don't you know, did anybody ever tell you that people with money have it because they hang onto it as long as possible.

Just pay it Kenneth, because I won't relax until you do.

Right, right, I'll go, I'll go and do it right now.

A Night in November

I drove past the Golf Club, in fact I drove past it five times and on the fifth time I drove home. Debrah was at aerobics, the kids were at their grannies. This gave me peace to work it all out, to work out the most exciting, totally outrageous crazy mad thing I had ever done in my life...300 pounds, I had for the half-year golf fees, one hundred pounds worth of electricity shares that my mother had bought me for my birthday, they could be worth 200 now...not enough...Christ, there must be something I could sell...the golf clubs must be worth at least 200 quid, I knew somebody in work who was looking to buy some...that would be enough, that would be just enough.

Every morning I woke up, I lay for five minutes asking myself "Are you sure, Kenneth, now, are you absolutely sure you know what you are doing", and the answer was always the same...too bloody right I do, in fact I can't wait.

Everything worked out so smoothly, no hitches.

...I sold the golf clubs and I threw in the bag and the trolley that Isobel and Ernie had bought and I got £300...and the electricity shares were wee buns and nobody knew a thing...it was then I knew what I was doing was destined.

The night before I could barely contain myself. I must not show any signs of unusual behaviour...I would fake falling asleep on the settee and Debrah would, as usual, leave me there and go to bed...but tonight, I was not asleep...I'd left work at lunch time and packed a small suitcase which I had hidden in the boot...I sat there watching the clock in the silence and never for one minute had doubts about what I was going to do...at six o'clock exactly I slipped quietly out of the house and into the car...as I was driving I felt I was like a car with no brakes speeding along, not to disaster...I was that car in Chitty Chitty Bang Bang when it came to the edge of the cliff, it took wings...that was me.

I crossed the Border for the first time in my life. It just never occurred to me to do it, we were taught to be afraid, to be afraid of the black magic, the dark evil, the mysterious jiggery Popery that'll brainwash us. But is that what it is? Is that what our leaders are really scared of, or is it that if the tables are turned they are afraid that we'll be treated the way we've treated the Taigs and we'll be the second-class citizens.

Yes, that could be part of it too, the fear of retribution - they say they are God-fearing men. What they fear is their own judgment day, their own behaviour staring them in the face.

A Night in November

Dublin airport, 10 kilometres, yes...*(Starts to sing to himself.)*...Trailer for Sale or Rent, Room to Let 50 Cents, No Phone No Pool No Pets, Ain't Got No Cigarettes...etc...etc...

I drove into the car park...it was a sight I'll never forget...the whole airport had been taken over by a green, white and gold army...there were check-ins going on in the car park...people were singing...at nine o'clock in the morning, they were singing and laughing and chanting "Ole, we're on our way, we're on our way to the USA."

So am I, I shouted...I am going to New York, hey, me too. I'm off to support Ireland in the World Cup, brill, isn't it, lads...I loved saying lads...like I was a comrade...like I was one of them...me and the lads...alright lads, eh...Italy, no problem...Ole Ole Ole.

I had forgotten myself, I was jumping up and down like a kid...a couple of lads started to laugh at my outburst, not in a mocking way...just as though they understood...yes everybody had a right to be happy that morning, everybody had their own story of how they got to be there...but at this moment in time, we were all the lads...and it felt good...people with streamers and hats and silly wigs and painted faces and I was part of them...Oh, if only Pauline could see me now.

Then I looked at myself...there I was standing out in the thousands like a sore thumb. I was dressed like this, God I looked like a right plonker...I looked more like the airport security...maybe that was why they were laughing at me...there was one man who was just standing smiling to himself...he was fifty if he was a day...had a look of respectability about him, he looked as uncomfortable in his World Cup T-shirt and his shorts and silly hat as I did in my Dunnes menswear gear...but like me he had the look of a man who was about to be set free.....we clocked each other and smiled.

Hey, mate, where do you get them T-shirts from.

What, the whole country is swamped with them, where have you been?

I've come from Belfast.

Oh, that's different.

He pulled the zip of his bag open and fumbled around and threw a T-shirt at me.

Here, for God's sake, put this on, you look like the man from the Welfare.

I laughed...I was, that's exactly who I was, but I wasn't telling him that.

Thanks mate...*(Puts on the T-shirt.)* How much do I owe you.

You can buy me a drink if I bump into you in New York.

I stripped off my shirt and tie and blazer, right there in the car park and put on the T-shirt...me standing in a green, white and orange shirt with a tricolour on it...unbelievable...unbelievable.

Myself and the man who give me the T-shirt made our way with the crowds to the terminal building.

Jasis, isn't this the business...isn't this what life is all about eh...would you look at us all...I tell you what, there is more borrowed money here than it took to crash Wall Street...ah, sure, if I hadn't done this I would regret it the rest of me life...much did you pay for your match ticket.

Oh, that, I haven't got that, sure I'll get it when I get there.

Are ye crazy or what...they will be selling at hundreds of dollars now...you have no chance.

Really...now I feel like a double plonker.

Tell you what, if we get split up I'll meet you in Eamon Doran's bar tonight on Second Avenue, I'm meetin' up with a few of the lads and we'll see what we can do, but I won't promise nothing...where are you stayin'?

What...am...Oh God, I didn't think about that.

You're well organised, aren't you...lukin like the rent man, no match tickets and nowhere to stay...what were you thinkin' of .

I got here and I'm going to America and I never thought further than that.

Yeah I know what you mean...You know two days ago I was sitting in me office looking out the window at the rain. There was me trussed up in me suit and tie, surrounded by other robots in suits and ties, and I looked out me window at a travel agents across the street. I see two lads kitted out in the team colours, and they bounced out waving their tickets and singing and cavorting. And I said to meself...excuse the language...but I said to meself, fuck it. I got up, lifted my briefcase and walked out the door. I said to my secretary "I'll see you when I see you,

I'm off to America to watch Ireland winning the World Cup" and here I am, on my way to the USA.

Me too, that's what I did. I just said fuck it too.

The name is Mick, meet me tonight in Eamon's and I'll see if I can get you a floor to crash on...It's great I haven't crashed on a floor since I was a student and do you know what...I'm lookin' forward to it.

Me too...by the way, I'm Kenneth.

No problem Kenneth.

Dead on, Mick...thanks, mate.

As I walked across the tarmac, my feet were not even touching the ground...don't look back, Kenneth, you've got this far, once you're on that jumbo, you can't get off, you are there, don't have no last minute twangs of conscience, just one and you're sunk. As I walked towards the flight I knew it could go either way, so I said leave it to fate, Kenneth, just leave it to the gods and see what happens when you reach the last step...let them decide, because at this point in time you are not of sound mind, you have no responsibility for yourself and I loved it...I reached the top, the attendant said good morning. I stopped, looked back, the fella behind me moved slightly, as if to let me wave to my loved ones in the viewing gallery...I looked, I was about to head down the gangway...and fate and the gods must have said to themselves...fuck it...and I burst out laughing and waved, then turned away into the unknown...I knew then that there was no turning back now for Kenneth Norman McCallister, for now I really was one of the lads.

The wife...?

It was the fella behind me..."Sorry"...I was still sniggering.

Waving to the wife?

No...just someone I knew...Kenneth, his name is.

My wife thinks I've gone to Lough Derg...but I have me face paints and a wig in case I'm caught by the cameras...bleeding RTE are everywhere.

Another pipes up.

I told my wife I was going fishing in Donegal. I told the bank manager I was building a garage and I told my boss in work I was going to

Grannie's funeral...So, when I come back I'd better have a couple of trout, build a garage and kill me Granny.

I'm alright, nobody will see me, we don't get RTE in Belfast, or at least not where I come from.

Yeah, you're like me, if Ireland win this match on Saturday I have to come home and pretend I'm not over the bleeding moon.

Do you live in Belfast too?

No, I work for a bleeding Italian restaurant.

A lad who sat beside me was well gone, he had almost demolished the contents of the duty free.

Were you at that match in Windsor Park?

I was.

I tell you what mate...he was speaking as he was trying to put his seat belt on to the other half of mine.

Ah, that's my seat belt.

He ignored me...you see you Belfast men, I am proud of yis, I am proud of the way, yis stood at Windsor Park and took what yis had to take and yis stood there...I didn't go...me...I was a coward...but I have to hand it to you...here, take a slug of that whiskey, because youse deserve a medal and Jackie's Army are proud of yis...*(Sings.)* We're all part of Jackie's Army...

No you wouldn't have been proud of me, you see, I'm a Protestant.

So am I.

Jesus, so he was...so he was and yet he said...God...you lucky bugger...so was he and yet...ah, what the hell...

Sure at the end of the day we are all part of Jackie's Army.

I took a slug of his whiskey and felt part of Jackie's Army too.

Then he sat staring at me.

Something wrong?

Something wrong?..Are you drinking that whiskey or makin' love to it.

Oh, yeah, thanks.

A Night in November

The flight across the Atlantic with Jackie's Army was something I could only ever have dreamed of. We sang and drank and carried on like we had been told these are your last hours on this planet...Everybody was part of Jackie's Army, the crew, the cock pit crew, the pilot...we were all the lads...Irish lads on our way to support our team...even the pilot was startin' the singsongs over the tannoy...the lad beside me wanted to send him up a drink but we had to draw the line somewhere. As the plane touched down in JFK there was an almighty roar of Ole Ole Ole...oh God, I was so deliriously happy...for a brief moment, I checked into my own head to see if there were any feelings of guilt or remorse or regret and I couldn't find one...I even thought because I couldn't find one like that then I should find thoughts of concern that I was selfish and heartless...but no...I knew I was on a road that had no turn-offs or roundabouts or even parking lay-bys...no, I must go until the end, what happens after that, who knows...and as I held onto the lad beside me, while me and his mate carried him off the plane...he was so drunk he couldn't remember the second line of Ole Ole Ole...as we carried him off I looked at him and thought, you're right mate, who cares, because however awful it is when I get to the end of it, I will always have the wonderful memory of being one of the lads *(Arms up in the air.)* Oh, sorry mate.

I'm in New York...I am in New York...I kept saying it over and over to myself...it's just like the TV...I felt part of a film set...yellow cabs, noise, Manhattan, millions all talking at once...I took a cab to Eamon Doran's bar to meet Mick...I didn't doubt for one minute that he wouldn't turn up...I was one of the lads and the lads all looked out for each other, I knew that instinctively...after thirty-four years of looking out for yourself, it was a lovely warm feeling of belongin'. This bar was just a continuation of the flight...wall to wall Irish men in green, white and gold still singing Ole, Ole, Ole...even the pilot was there...it looked like total chaos and mayhem...people making phone calls from numbers they were given back in Ireland, somebody vaguely knew someone who might have floor space.

Hello, I'm saying hello, my name's Kevin, you know my cousin Robbie Hagan, don't you...no, you do...yes, sure you grew up together before you emigrated...in Cavan, yes...yes, I know it was 35 years ago. I know you were only five, but he said that you said that if he was ever in America to look you up...well, he's not here, so he said for me to phone you and see if you have a floor I could crash on, seeing as I'm here instead of him and I'm his cousin and you know him and I'm from

A Night in November

Cavan too...terrific mate...I have a mate...great, hey...there's a boy here with space for two more.

It was as if all these people knew each other...I suppose this must go back to the Famine. Irish people landing here and herded into sheds and then sent out into the unknown to fend for themselves...I suppose from that day on it was the unspoken rule that the Irish would have to look after their own...even me, even me who never considered himself an Irishman ...in their eyes I was one of them...and I loved it.

Kenny...Kenny.

It was Mick.

He looked twenty years younger than he looked in Dublin airport, his silly hat and shorts and T-shirt now seemed absolutely right and he knew it.

Here, take this address and number, you have floor space for as long as you like...no luck with the tickets, but sure some of the lads were saying you'd be as well off watching it here, for the stadium will be like a chip pan, sure the crack will be mighty.

That'll suit me Mick...and thank you very much for everything you've done for me...as soon as I said it, I knew it sounded like a line from a Helen Steiner Rice get well card...but what the hell.

Well, me and Mick and some of the lads partied to the wee small hours in Eamon Doran's bar...every now and then I would nip down to the loo, look in the mirror to see if it was me...*(Reads his T-shirt in the mirror.)* elo, elo, elo, elo...laugh, then take the stairs four at a time back to my fellow Irishmen at the bar.

...And from that day on he always kept the chickens in the loft...

The next day - the day of the match against Italy, the temperature was 98 degrees in the shade.

(Sings as he changes into World Cup gear.) We're all part of Jackie's Army, we're going to the USA and we'll really shake them up, when we win the World Cup, cause Ireland are the greatest football team.

The atmosphere in Eamon Doran's was bloody electric...the bar was jammed with men and women...buzzin' with the kind of excitement I hadn't felt since I was a kid...and the women...just as knowledgeable about their team as the men...now, that did surprise me...I mean, women and football...

On your own, handsome?

Me.

Aye, you...standing there like the Tom that got the cat.

You mean cream...Oh no, what a stupid thing to say.

What?

You mean like the cat that got the cream...Oh Kenneth, just shut up.

What fecking use is a bowl of cream when you're dying for a shag.

What?

Ah, sure I'm only slaggin'...want to join us...we're over here.

I looked over and there was at least ten of them...God...me and all those women...am...oh God...I was scared...

Come on, we won't ate ye...well, not unless you're desperate...

What's your name?

Kenneth.

Girls, this is Kenneth, he prefers ating ice cream to shaggin'.

Dirty laughs all round...I can see I'm not going to come out of this one alive.

Packie Bonner, I want to have your babies.

It was a man said that.

The team were on the pitch.

(Kenneth reacts as he hears the Irish National Anthem sung by everyone in the pub...He eventually rises, at first nervously and then defiantly.)

(Girls' voices.)

I don't think Andy Townsend should have tipped his hair...he doesn't suit it.

You should talk, look at that temperature, it must be 120 degrees out there. It's not fair, our lads have to play in that and look at them Italians all dead cocky because they're used to it, I hope you all get sunburnt.

Come on lads *(Sings as girls.)* We love you boys in green, we love you boys in green,...sing Kenneth.

I don't know it.

Jasis, there's only one fecking line.

They sang it in my ear...each song in turn to teach me...to help me to be a part of them...I remembered that night in Windsor Park when I sang the Sash into that man's ear, so he could be part of us...to be part of us, so he could be safe from us...And then suddenly a deafening roar and I'm grabbed by at least six of the women.

What, what happened...A goal.

Jesus, we scored...

(Sings.) Stick your pizzas up your arse...come on Kenneth.

I don't know it.

Join in the chorus.

Stick your pizzas up your arse.

Why do all the songs have one line.

So, they're easy to remember when you're drunk.

The man who wanted to have Packie's babies now wanted to have Ray Houghton's, he was delirious.

God, I wouldn't have missed this for the world.

Come on lads. The second half started and Ireland were still ahead...

Oh...No...Ah...get back...oh...ah...oo ah Paul McGrath

And I wanted to have Paul McGrath's babies.

And then...and then...and then...the final whistle.

(Kenneth is delirious.)

We all piled onto Second Avenue and stopped the traffic...everyone just standing in the middle of the road...as the horns tooted and the traffic came to a standstill...nothing barrin' an earthquake stops traffic in America but we did, with our one-line songs...that's all it took...there were lads sitting on bonnets of cars...just singing and cheering and

A Night in November

oblivious to the chaos it was causing...no tonight on Second Avenue, New York, it was our night.

I thought back to Windsor Park...I thought of those angry men and their Trick or Treat and their cold staring eyes and their hard bitter faces and I thought to myself Jerry was right...what a pity, what a shame that they can't allow themselves to be a part of this...what a terrible pity.

At one stage the police were called...expecting to find crazed drunken Irishmen about to wreck all around them...oh yes, they had heard of these wild untamable mad men and they came prepared, batons at the ready, armoured vans sitting in waiting...what a shock for these poor men and women of the NYPD.

Look out boys, it's the peelers.

Move to the sidewalk, immediately.

No problem, officer. Say officer, could me and some of the lads have our photographs taken with you. You see no-one is going to believe we were in America and we couldn't be arsed to go all the way to the Statue of Liberty.

Sure just give me a minu...

Great lads, he says, it's okay, everybody back.

No, I didn't mean...

You're a smasher, you are, you're just like that big fella in the Miami Vice, isn't he, smile...*(Sings.)* We love you boys in blue, we love you boys in blue - God, we loved beating the Italians.

I was singing at the top of my voice..."Stick your pizzas up your arse"...everybody took it in good stead, even the Italian policeman... well, almost...I stopped to get my breath and a drink when this policeman came over to me.

Where are you from in Ireland?

Me...Belfast...I am an Irishman from Belfast...I was enjoying saying that.

It's just been on the news, there was a dreadful shooting near Belfast tonight.

What...where...

Some guys were watching the match when a couple of gunmen came in and shot dead six of them...

I watched this wild and wonderful harmless celebration of human beings just simply bringing out the best in themselves...just a parade of the best there is in human nature and tried to connect it with the worst...impossible...just impossible.

What's up with ye mate.

It was Mick, back from the match and as happy as I'd ever seen a person.

I told him what had happened back home.

He put his arm around my shoulder and pulled me into him...another man has never done that to me, but it was right for Mick to do it...he knew what I felt. Mick and I had shared something, we had both said Fuck It in our lives and we were mates.

Come on in and have a drink Mick...I want you to drink with me, because tonight I can stand here and tell you that I am no part of the men who did that...I am not of them anymore...no, no-one can point the finger at Kenneth Norman McCallister and say, these people are part of you...tonight I absolve myself...I am free of them Mick...I am free of it, I am a free man...I am a Protestant Man, I'm an Irish Man.

THE END